# CONTENTS

N

W

E

S

# ARCHITECTURAL BEGINNINGS

When Captain Arthur Phillip sailed into Botany Bay, on the east coast of Australia, in January 1788, he was unimpressed. The bay was unprotected and shallow and surrounded by poor soil and its shore was observed to be unproductive with scarce fresh water. Having led a fleet of ships halfway around the world to found a penal colony for British convicts, he decided to explore further north for a better location.

He found it just 12 kilometres up the coast. Port Jackson was an inlet discovered and named by Captain James Cook in 1770 although it was not extensively explored at the time. What Phillip found as he ventured up the inlet was, in his opinion, 'the finest harbour in the world'.

Named after the British Home Secretary Thomas Townshend (Lord Sydney), Sydney Cove was a well sheltered deep water anchorage with ample fresh water supplies. It was a perfect site for the first official British settlement on the Australian continent.

T0363238

3

**FOR THE FIRST TWO DECADES OF SYDNEY'S EXISTENCE THE COLONY WAS SO LACKING IN APPROPRIATE SKILLS AND TOOLS THAT THE MAJORITY OF BUILDINGS CONSTRUCTED WERE OF POOR QUALITY AND IN NEED OF CONSTANT MAINTENANCE.**

The situation changed dramatically with the appointment of Major-General Lachlan Macquarie as Governor of New South Wales in 1810. Finding many structures throughout the settlement in a 'most ruinous state of decay', Macquarie implemented a set of building codes that dictated a minimum standard for any future construction. Teaming up with convicted forger and architect Francis Greenway, the Governor also commissioned a series of classically inspired public buildings including Hyde Park Barracks (1819) and St James Church (1824), both of which still stand today.

From the mid to late 19th century architectural trends in Sydney closely followed those adopted throughout the British Empire. Grand classical revival styles were used extensively for public and administrative buildings whilst well to do residents displayed their wealth with elaborate Victorian Italianate or sober Georgian home designs.

# THE RISE OF MODERNISM

As the 20th century dawned worldwide architectural fashions continued to make their way into Sydney's built environment, particularly during the interwar years (1919-1939). Many commercial buildings adopted the sleek Art Deco and Moderne aesthetics from Europe (David Jones Building, 1938) whilst others attempted to emulate the soaring skyscraper designs of New York and Chicago (AWA Tower, 1939).

These new styles did not, however, entirely sweep away the architectural past as many administrative and commercial buildings were still being designed in what is now termed Free Classical, complete with all the traditional motifs and orders seen throughout the 19th century.

Times were rapidly changing however and the wave of International Modernism that was transforming both architectural form and theory throughout world would inevitably reach the shores of Australia.

Although the movement had its beginnings in Europe during the early 1920s it did not make a significant impact on Australian cities until after the Second World War when architects including Robin Boyd in Melbourne and Harry Seidler in Sydney introduced Modernist architecture to the nation's built environment. Seidler's commercial work in particular (Australia Square Tower, 1967; MLC Centre, 1977) had an enormous impact on Sydney's CBD from the 1960s through to the 90s.

Many of his buildings
have become icons of Australian
Modernist architecture and,
along with Boyd's Melbourne
residential work, represent
a unique regional take on
Modernist ideals and practices.

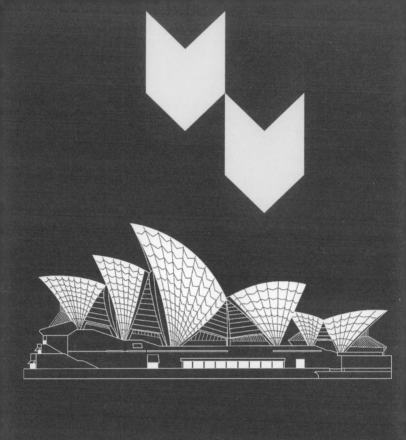

# SYDNEY OPERA HOUSE

Arguably the most recognised built symbol of Australia, the Sydney Opera House is one of Modernism's great sculptural achievements.

Calls for a dedicated opera house began in the late 1940s, led by the Director of the NSW State Conservatorium of Music Eugene Goossens. The main venue for large theatrical performances at the time, Sydney Town Hall, was increasingly considered inadequate and on 13 September 1955 NSW Premier Joseph Cahill launched an international design competition for a new venue. In 1957 Danish architect Jorn Utzon was announced as the winner and construction began in 1959 on Bennelong Point. The structure was built in three stages: stage one (1959-63) saw the construction of the upper podium; stage two (1963-67) the outer concrete shells; stage three (1967-73) interior design and construction.

The iconic roof shells went through numerous iterations between 1957 and 1963 before Utzon and his engineer, Ove Arup, devised a form (utilising computer aided structural analysis) that was workable from both an engineering and financial point of view.

The Sydney Opera House was formally opened on 20 October 1973, almost 20 years after it was originally conceived. The podium base is clad in locally sourced pink granite whilst the shell forms or 'sails' (actually precast concrete panels supported by ribs) are covered in 1,056,006 glossy white and matte cream tiles. The entire venue has a capacity for 5,738 people in six different spaces with the main concert hall able to hold 2,679 patrons.

Utzon died on 29 November 2008 but lived to witness the listing of the Sydney Opera House as a UNESCO World Heritage Site on 28 June 2007.

## ✪ OF NOTE

### Tom Bass Sculpture 'Research' / 1959

Walking back towards Circular Quay will take you past
the Bennelong Apartment complex. Between the two
buildings is a stone staircase (Moore Steps, 1868) leading to
Macquarie Street. To the right of the stairs, on the apartment wall,
sits a dynamic piece of artwork by Australian sculptor Tom Bass.
It was commissioned by chemical company ICI for the curtain
wall office building constructed on this site in 1957
(Bates Smart & McCutcheon, demolished 1996).

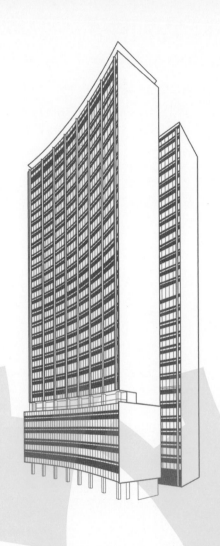

# AMP BUILDING

Towering above Circular Quay the AMP building, along with nearby Gold Fields House, formed the modern 'gateway to Sydney' in the 1960s, defining the height of the city's skyscrapers until the 1980s. At 26 storeys (115 metres) the podium and tower design took the mantle of Australia's tallest building from Melbourne's ICI House (20 storeys, 1958) while using that building's precedent to break Sydney's height limit regulations (a 150 foot limit placed on city buildings in 1912).

Constructed as the new headquarters for the Australian Mutual Provident Society (a financial services company formed in 1849) the AMP Building consists of a five-storey podium supporting a 21 storey tower, sited on a large pedestrian plaza. The aluminium curtain wall is acutely defined by bronze coloured spandrels and intersecting expressed mullion elements with a further narrow band of bronze panels running across the glazing, breaking up the regular grid pattern. An increased sense of verticality is achieved in the tower design with the curtain wall sectioned into seven bays by eight narrow marble panelled columns. Extending from the base to the top, these align with the supporting columns rising from the podium structure. The overall design distinguishes itself from many other contemporary curtain wall buildings with the gentle curvature of the facade, a feature which, along with its height, caused a surprising level of controversy at the time of construction.

Although the internal office spaces have been remodelled since construction, the foyers are largely intact and still display the original marble dressing and stainless steel columns. On the Western (Young Street) facade there is a sculpture by artist Tom Bass. It depicts the goddess of Peace and Plenty flanked by the male figure of Labour on the left and a wife and child on the right. Underneath is the AMP corporation's Latin motto; "Amicus certus in re incerta" ("A certain friend in uncertain times") which, along with the three figures, could be found on many AMP buildings from the 19th century onwards.

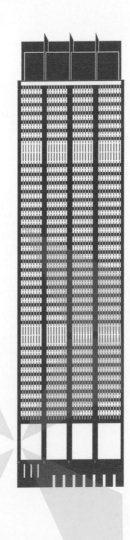

# GOVERNOR PHILLIP TOWER

Topping out at 227 metres Governor Phillip Tower is the third tallest building in Sydney and is located on one of Australia's most important National Heritage sites. Shortly after establishment of the new settlement of Sydney in January 1788 a building was constructed on what is now the corner of Bridge and Phillip Streets to serve as the residence for the first Governor of New South Wales, Captain Arthur Phillip. This first Government House, made of English bricks and local stone, was gradually extended and repaired by a succession of eight Governors, eventually being replaced by a new, grander structure (located near the Royal Botanic Gardens) in 1845. Demolished in 1846 the original site remained untouched until the 1980s when the present office tower was proposed for the site. Concerned heritage groups urged the NSW Government to allow archaeological exploration of the site before construction commenced and subsequent discoveries of well-preserved foundations and artefacts resulted in a re-design of the tower to preserve the findings.

Designed by Melbourne firm Denton Corker Marshall, Governor Phillip Tower forms part of a larger complex that includes Governor Macquarie Tower, First Government House Plaza and the Museum of Sydney. Sitting on a sandstone podium four storeys above street level the height of the tower is further enhanced by massive zinc-plated transfer beams that elevate the occupied floors a further six levels. The surface is clad in a flush finish of granite and glass that bestows a high quality, expensive quality upon the facades. The steel blade forms topping the roof, something of a Denton Corker Marshall design signature, have been nick-named the 'milk crate' by Sydneysiders.

The remains of First
Government House (located
under what is now First
Government House Plaza)
are partly visible through
a glass pyramid in front
of the entrance to the
Museum of Sydney, all of
which has been integrated
into a modern office complex
in what many consider
a respectful manner.

# LINER HOUSE

Constructed as the Australian headquarters for the Wilh. Wilhelmson Agency (Norway's largest shipping company at the time) Liner House was proof that new commercial Modernist architecture could exist in harmony with existing buildings.

Instead of exploiting the site for maximum financial return the company decided to have a building designed entirely for its own use, constructed to a height that was within the scale of its immediate neighbours. Comprising a ground floor, mezzanine and four upper floors the building is set back 1.2 metres from the adjacent building facades. The curtain wall, composed of aluminium-framed windows with blue ceramic spandrel panels, is expressed horizontally by projecting sunshades with the top floor being further delineated by a framework form. In keeping with the sympathetic urban nature of the building's English Portland stone (complementing the stone used on the adjoining buildings) was used for the external flanking walls and ground floor.

Internally, Liner House still retains many of its original fittings including a spiral staircase and mural screen made of brass, copper, aluminium and stainless steel elements by Australian sculptor Douglas Annand.

In 1961 the building was awarded the prestigious Sulman Medal in recognition of its 'consistent honesty in design and good taste for this building' and 'very good manners to its neighbours'.

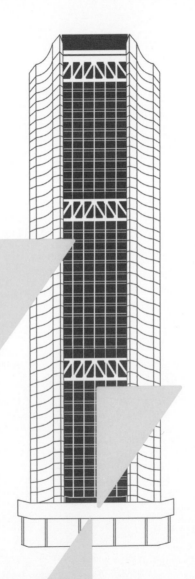

# SUNCORP PLACE

Originally designed for Qantas, the building now known as Suncorp Place was begun in 1970 but, due to union delays, wasn't completed until 1982. Realised well into the post-modern era the structure can be read as a soft fusion of late Brutalism and Hi-tech architectural styles.

Broad raw concrete columns, angled to form an elongated hexagon, flank curtain walls on each elevation. Each glazed facade is separated into three segments by horizontal concrete truss structures; functional features that express engineering form.

The building is topped by a steel cage structure that adds 18 metres to the height of Suncorp Place, making it 204 metres tall.

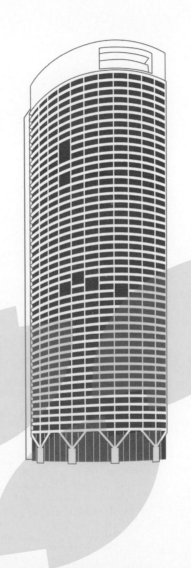

# GROSVENOR PLACE

Completed in the year Australia celebrated its bicentennial, Grosvenor Place exhibits many of the regional design aspects and signature features that Harry Seidler had been developing and incorporating into his commercial work since the 1960s. The 44 floor tower is made up of two crescent-shaped halves encasing an elliptical central core, lending a unique form to the structure that can be seen as an evolution of Seidler's previous cylindrical shaped Australia Square and MLC buildings. The curved form, along with large column-free floor plates, also provides tenants with unmatched panoramic views of Sydney Harbour.

The granite-clad facade incorporates sunshades at varying angles that, along with the use of high performance thermal glazing, minimise the effects of harsh sunlight on the interiors. The sunshade elements also add textural interest to the building's surface, a practice which Siedler was fond of utilising on many of his projects, differentiating them from the usual plain Modernist grids and flush finishes.

Entry to the building is through a spectacular lobby space that expresses the curved forms of the main structure in many of its elements. Displayed on the walls of the central lift core are large artworks by American minimalist artist Frank Stella. Seidler was a big believer in large buildings as venues for the display of art and the geometry of Grosvenor Place was apparently partly inspired by Stella's work.

Forming a prominent transition between the historical Rocks area and the modern CBD, Grosvenor Place represents the continuing impact that Siedler's work had on Sydney's built environment throughout the late 20th century.

# UNDER
# THREAT

Demolition
is imminent.

# SIRIUS APARTMENTS

Named after the flagship of the First Fleet that sailed into Sydney harbour in 1788, the Sirius apartment complex was built by the NSW Housing Commission to re-house public tenants of Millers Point. Throughout the 1960s and 70s heritage groups and local residents teamed up with unions to fight the NSW government's re-development proposals which would see the demolition of significant numbers of historic buildings to make way for high rise apartments and hotels.

Both the Rocks and Millers Point had long been home to a population of underprivileged and increasingly ageing residents reliant on government housing and it was the desire to enable these vulnerable people to remain in their community, whilst maintaining the working class nature of the area, that prompted the union led Green Bans of the 1970s. Although the preservation of the built heritage was really secondary to this aim the resulting planning compromises ensured that many buildings were saved.

Comprised of stacked rectangular blocks the Sirius apartment building rises and falls in an almost organic manner, as if following the topography of the landscape. The pod-like nature of the components and the raw concrete finish (the original plan to paint the building white was scrapped due to budget constraints) reflect similar projects from 1960s and 70s Japan, particularly the work of Metabolist architects such as Kiyonori Kikutake. The building was designed for both aged and family residents, providing a total of 79 one, two, three and four bedroom apartments throughout the complex.

Although listed by the National Trust as a significant example of late Brutalism, the fate of the apartments has lately been sealed. Most of the residents have been relocated by Housing NSW in anticipation of the imminent demolition and redevelopment of the site.

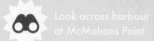

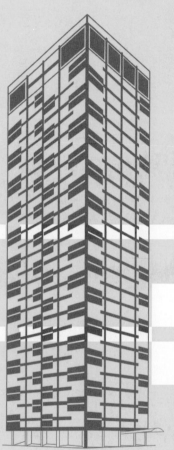

# BLUES POINT TOWER

Seidler's first major high rise project, Blues Point Tower has attracted an inordinate amount of criticism from Sydneysiders since its completion. In 1957 McMahons Point, now one of Sydney's most exclusive harbour-side suburbs, was being considered for industrial rezoning, motivating Seidler to put forward an alternative, and very Modernist, residential proposal. Reflecting architect Le Corbusier's theories regarding the future development of dense urban forms, Seidler planned a series of 28 high-rise towers for the area, all surrounded by landscaped gardens and commanding harbour views. Although the industrial rezoning ideas quickly fell out of favour any initial enthusiasm for the apartment project also rapidly waned and by 1962 Seidler had only managed to have one tower realised.

Rising 25 floors (Australia's tallest residential building until 1970) the tower is square in plan with brick clad facades and features interesting surface patterning. On the East-West elevations each floor is expressed by ribbon windows flanked by staggered balconies alternating on the right and left sides. The North-South facades have a similar layout with additional balcony elements running staggered up the middle. This aversion to unbroken symmetrical grids became a signature Seidler element and can be found on many of his subsequent tower projects.

From the beginning Blues Point Tower was decried by many as an eyesore completely at odds with its surroundings. In a Modernist sense, however, it should be considered an unmitigated success; A vertical urban form rising amongst the trees and lawns of Blues Point as a free-standing sculpture. As Seidler himself said: "I've always thought Blues Point Tower is one of my best buildings and I stand by that. Anybody who can't see anything in it ought to go back to school."

# UNDER THREAT

Redevelopment is imminent.

36

# GOLD FIELDS HOUSE

Designed by the same architectural firm that produced the AMP Building, Gold Fields House (commissioned by British mining company Consolidated Gold Fields) demonstrates the evolution of the curtain wall throughout Australia during the 1960s. The coloured glass spandrels and light aluminium mullions have been replaced with composite materials and heavier forms, lending a more solid expressive appearance to the facades. Although reclad in the 1990s the building retains the original dimensions and contrasts of the grid form; wide spandrel bands running parallel to the ribbon windows are intersected with narrow strips at four pane intervals. The windows in each section are further divided equally by an opaque flush panel.

Gold Fields House was one of a series of freestanding skyscrapers that transformed Sydney's skyline in the 1960s and stands today as a neat, well-proportioned example of mid-century corporate architecture. Unfortunately it may soon be transformed beyond recognition having being purchased in 2014 with the intention of redevelopment into luxury accommodation.

# 51 PITT ST

Located on a corner site this 11 storey office building is a generally typical example of late 1950s curtain wall commercial design, with a couple of quirks. Two window rows in from the corner the Pitt Street facade extends outwards, coming in line with the adjacent building. The Dalley Street facade wraps around into the rear lane, giving the impression of a free-standing, full curtain wall structure. This is for effect only, however, as the windows terminate after two rows, the remaining wall taking the form of a brick warehouse. The facades themselves are made up of light blue spandrels separated by unbroken aluminium mullion fins, all of which sit above a colonnaded ground floor.

Overall the exterior of 51 Pitt Street is intact and, apart from the ground floor entrance level, is in quite original condition.

# AUSTRALIA SQUARE

When completed in 1967 the Australia Square complex (comprising a 170 metre tower and 13 floor building, both sited on an open plaza) represented a new form of urban development in an Australian city. Occupying an entire city block (made possible by the acquisition and demolition of around 30 properties) the project sought to provide a less congested environment for city workers and pedestrians, being an early example of publically accessible open space situated on private land.

Construction commenced in 1962, the 13 floor Plaza Building on Pitt Street being completed first in order to provide rental income whilst the tower was constructed. Raised on angled concrete piloti the Plaza Building encloses one end of the space as well as defining the street edge.

Sited at the opposite end of the plaza is Australia Square Tower, a building regarded as one of Harry Seidler's greatest works of commercial architecture. In association with engineer Pier Luigi Nervi (known as the Italian god of concrete), Seidler devised the unique cylindrical form for both practical and aesthetic reasons. Given the relatively narrow site and council rules around building setbacks a circular design provided more floorplate space and occupied less of the site compared to a traditional rectangular building, in addition to providing better outward views. The structural nature of the building (a central round core with external structural columns) also results in uncluttered office space. Visually, the external column fins soaring past the prominent spandrel bands, draw the eye dramatically up the tower, at the top of which sits a revolving restaurant. The lobby interior is no less spectacular with its celling of interlocking ribs and colourful mural by New York artist Sol LeWitt wrapping around the central core.

Australia Square Tower is considered a milestone building in Australia's Modernist architectural history. Architectural photographer Patrick Bingham-Hall calls it "Australia's finest tall building, a perfect resolution of rational geometry, structural ingenuity and heroic form".

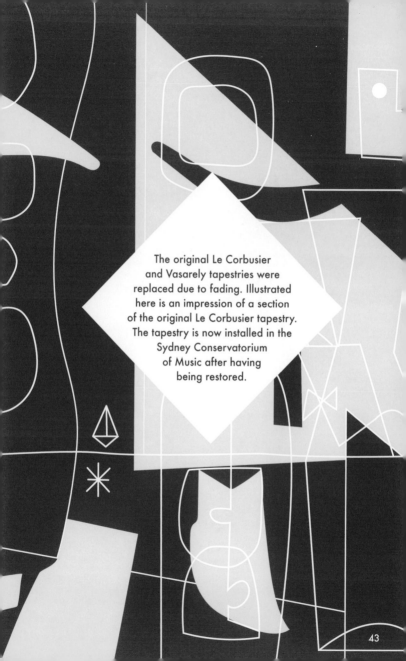

The original Le Corbusier and Vasarely tapestries were replaced due to fading. Illustrated here is an impression of a section of the original Le Corbusier tapestry. The tapestry is now installed in the Sydney Conservatorium of Music after having being restored.

# GUARDIAN ASSURANCE BUILDING

The early 1960s curtain wall design of this building demonstrates the tendency of architects at the time to develop a more 'expressive' form. The windows and spandrel elements are encased in a projecting grid which is itself framed in an expressed rectangle. The overall appearance is a little fussy and can be read as a transition between the clean aluminium and glazed skin of early International Style designs and the later, composite 'punched window' styles.

Originally constructed for the British Guardian Assurance Company (now AXA) the building was recently transformed into the Tank Stream boutique hotel. Apart from the addition of four extra floors the exterior form of the building was generally retained including the original cladding of locally sourced Wombeyan marble (no longer quarried). The hotel is named after the stream (now part of the sewerage system running under the city) that provided the early European settlers of Sydney with fresh water.

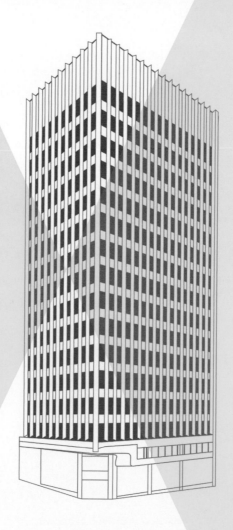

# CURRENCY HOUSE

Located in a prime CBD location on the corner of Pitt and Hunter Streets, Currency House appears ostensibly to be a typical early 1970s composite curtain wall design. On closer inspection however the overall facade treatment alludes more to the machine age forms of Art Deco architecture.

The triangular mullion elements run the length of the building, terminating past the top floor windows and providing a repetitive serrated edge pattern when viewed from street level. The spandrels display equally repetitive patterns of lines which add to the decorative verticality of the design. Clad in tan coloured composite stone Currency House presents as a well-proportioned and subtly elegant structure that sets itself apart other office buildings of the era.

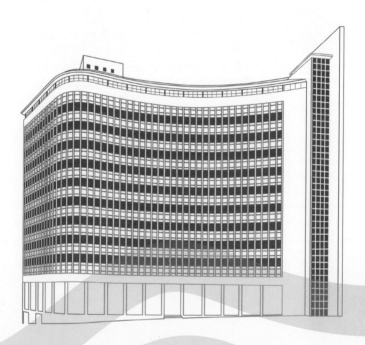

# QANTAS HOUSE

Officially opened by Prime Minister Robert Menzies on October 28th, 1957, Qantas House was the first purpose-built headquarters for what was then known as Qantas Empire Airways, Australia's sole international airline.

The third oldest airline in the world (established in 1920 as 'Queensland and Northern Territory Aerial Services Limited'), Qantas had greatly expanded its services in the post war years and by the 1950s was flying to multiple destinations around the globe. The international nature of the business was reflected in the International Style of the new building with its use of a broad aluminium and glass curtain wall, increasingly utilised at the time as the face of corporate architecture throughout the world.

What distinguishes Qantas House from other contemporary office designs is the form the architects used to express this new engineering technology. The facade follows the curved edge of Chifley Square, wrapping around to meet Hunter Street before terminating at Emil Sodersten's 1936 City Mutual Life Building. The green glazing and deep blue enamelled spandrels are intersected by aerofoil shaped aluminium mullions, all of which are framed by a contrasting border of local sandstone. Located above the sandstone band is a recessed rooftop level that originally contained staff and recreational facilities. The 11 office levels sit above a double height foyer clad in polished black granite with large, bronze-framed windows.

Judged the best new building in the British Commonwealth by the Royal Institute of British Architects in 1959, Qantas House is still regarded as one of Sydney's finest curtain wall designs of the 1950s and is currently listed on the NSW State Heritage Register.

# PEARL ASSURANCE BUILDING

Originally constructed for the Pearl Assurance Company of London, 1 Castlereagh Street is a neatly designed office building with an interesting surface treatment. The ground and first levels are set back to form a colonnade above which the building rises 20 floors.

The mullion elements, faced with cream marble, provide a stark contrast to the dark bronze stone cladding (locally quarried polished trachyte) of the spandrels and columns. The aluminium framed windows project beyond the spandrels and the use of dark glazing further enhances the overall contrasting quality of the facade surfaces.

The building was one of the first in Sydney to incorporate new window technology that enabled each panel to pivot around an axis, allowing easy cleaning from the inside. In addition, internal venetian blinds were sandwiched between the double glazing of each panel.

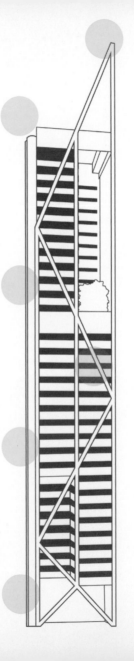

# CAPITA CENTRE

Although constrained by a tight, restricted site Harry Seidler managed to produce a building expressing many of his design hallmarks that would otherwise require a much larger space. The architect used the irregular site shape to his advantage by placing the core and main lift shaft at the perimeter, leaving a clear rectangular space for the tower.

This provided more open, flexible floor space on each level than would be possible with a central core. Creating voids throughout the structure also enabled maximum natural light to penetrate the floors, starting with the publically accessible open space at ground level.

The trade-off for all this, however, was a reduction in overall lateral stiffness which resulted in what is probably the most dramatic structural feature of the building, the exposed truss on the facade. A zig-zag framed in vertical elements, the truss soars up the tower carrying the eye through the alternating spaces of voids and louvered surfaces.

Terminating at a flag pole (which brings the height of the building to 183 metres) this external support feature places the Capita Centre firmly in the High-Tech Structural Expressionist school of modern architecture.

# MLC CENTRE

Completed exactly ten years after his seminal Australia Square project, Seidler's MLC Centre saw an evolution and refining of the architect's urban planning ideas. Teaming up once again with Italian engineer Pier Luigi Nervi (whose beautiful concrete geometric patterns can be seen in the ceilings of many of the structures), Seidler designed an open plaza comprising a 67 storey tower surrounded by retail, arts and recreation facilities, reflecting his belief in providing uncongested central urban space for city workers and pedestrians. The tower has an octagonal floorplan with a central core and is structurally supported by eight massive external columns that taper towards the top of the building. The office windows are recessed from the horizontal beam spandrels, providing both sun shading and a heavier textural quality to the surface. As it only occupies 20 percent of the site, the tower (Australia's tallest building until 1985) seems an integral, not over-bearing, feature of the complex.

The plaza is arranged on podiums of differing levels on which are placed various structures, circular in form, that relate spatially to the tower in an almost organic manner. A large central well admits natural light to the shopping arcades below whilst the distinctive mushroom shaped structure on the North East corner is home to the Commercial Travellers' Association's Business Club. The Theatre Royal, Australia's oldest theatrical institution, is also part of the complex, the original theatre building (opened in 1875) having been demolished, along with the Australia Hotel (1889), to clear the site for the MLC Centre. As with all of Seidler's commercial projects, contemporary artwork features prominently and includes the bright yellow 'S' sculpture by Charles Perry (located on the top level of the piazza) and "New Constellation", by Robert Owen (hanging on the tower foyer wall).

A thriving hub in Sydney's business precinct, the MLC Centre was further confirmation of Harry Seidler's pre-eminence as a designer of finely crafted and sensitive built forms within often harsh and uncompromising urban environments.

59

# RESERVE BANK BUILDING

Established as Australia's central bank on 14th of January, 1960, construction of a new Sydney office for the Reserve Bank commenced in 1961. The bank's administrators made it clear that the new design should be contemporary and international, reflecting the post-war cultural shifts of the nation. They also insisted on the use of high quality Australian sourced materials for construction and Australian art for decoration. The resulting design comprised a four-storey podium topped by a sixteen-storey tower. The double height ground level, entered via a granite terrace, is recessed and fully glazed whilst the two floors above project outwards on horizontal platforms.

The tower is composed of curtain wall facades clad with locally sourced black granite mullions and cream marble spandrels (4 panels each). Square aluminium windows puncture the surface and are recessed for sun shading, with additional projecting shades on the west elevation. At the top level are eight bays defined by the extended granite mullion elements which in turn become column supports.

Apart from furnishings and some fittings the foyer interior is largely original. Eight gold anodised-metal panels line the ceiling and the rear wall, clad in the same Wombeyan marble as the exterior, is decorated with an abstract sculpture by Bim Hilder. Another sculpture by Australian-American artist Margel Hinder sits in the Martin Place forecourt.

Sydney Law School Building / 1969 / 173 Philip Street

Sitting opposite the Law Courts building on Phillip Street is an earlier, far more expressive example of Brutalist architecture. Columns stack up the facades like blocks delineating the location of each floor. The windows, grouped into sets of four over a shared projecting spandrel, are shaded with horizontal fin elements that alternate in spacing from the lower floors to the top. Constructed as Sydney University's law faculty campus, the school has now relocated to a new building and, at the time of writing, the Philip Street structure was slated for demolition.

Utilising locally produced materials and art the Reserve Bank building demonstrated both Australian technological and cultural prowess that, in turn, reflected a heightened notion of self-reliance and confidence that was being felt in the post-war years.

The sense that the nation was now an independent, mature country, free from any colonial ties, was further enhanced by the change from British derived pounds, shillings and pence to a decimal currency system in 1966, all overseen, of course, by the Reserve Bank of Australia.

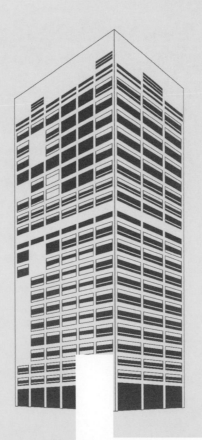

# LAW COURTS BUILDING

Housing the High and Federal Courts of Australia and the Supreme Court of NSW, the Law Courts building is a strong, sober design that befits its crucial role in Australia's legal system. The building's prestige is further emphasised by its location on Queens Square, around which some of Sydney's earliest administrative and civic architecture stands, including the Mint (1816), St James Church (1824) and the old Supreme Court building (1828).

The building is a prime example of the Brutalist style as it had developed in Australia throughout the late 1960s and 70s, particularly when applied to administrative and academic architecture. Clad in pre-cast concrete, the facades are lifted three storeys above the entrance foyer on slim columns before settling into a pattern of strip windows and blank panels. This informs the function of the internal spaces as open offices and closed courtrooms, with added textural interest provided by horizontal concrete sunshades.

A building that clearly demonstrates its purpose whilst responding to local environmental conditions, the Law Courts building is a typically pragmatic expression of 1970s regional Brutalist architecture.

# CENTREPOINT

At 309 metres (including spire) Sydney Tower is the city's tallest freestanding structure. Sitting above the Westfield shopping centre building, construction of the tower commenced in 1975 and it was opened to the public in 1981. The supporting shaft consists of 46 barrel-shaped units (each weighing 27 tonnes) topped by the multi-level turret structure.

The welded steel frame turret was fabricated at the base and gradually raised to the top as construction of the shaft proceeded. Braced by 56 steel cables, forming a hyperboloid shape, the tower was designed to withstand winds in excess of 260kph and includes a 162,000 litre water tank in the turret to serve as a counterbalance. The 'golden basket' as it is known has a capacity for 960 people and includes an observation deck, two revolving restaurants, and two active telecommunication transmission levels.

A further external viewing platform above the turret, added in 2005, provides an extra thrill for those with the nerve.

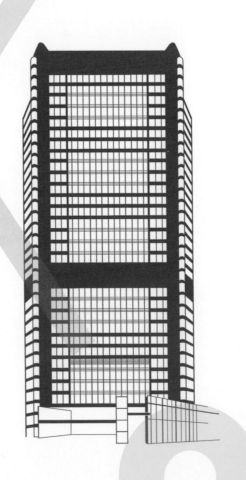

# KING GEORGE BUILDING

Now referred to simply as 388 George Street, the building situated on one of Sydney's busiest intersections has long been regarded as an iconic example of 1970s Brutalist/High Tech architecture. Triangular in shape, the three glass facades are flanked by circular stairway and lift cores, dramatically expressed externally in off-form concrete. To provide relief from the harsh solar conditions Andrews applied a system of polycarbonate sunshades hung off an intricate space frame lattice, giving the glazed facades what many considered a lively and delicate quality that relieved somewhat the harsh structural concrete finishes. Renovations during the 1990s, however, saw the removal of the lattice frame system, partly to satisfy the new tenants' (NRMA Insurance) desire for increased natural light and unimpeded city views. Environmental control is now performed by sensor-equipped glass panels which help ventilate the five sky gardens (expressed on the facade as five aluminium-framed rectangles) incorporated into the new design.

What some see as a degradation of the building's original unique character, others consider an appropriate renewing and upgrading of a technological system, allowing a significant architectural example to exist in an overall intact form for many years to come.

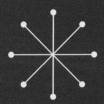

# COMMONWEALTH BANK BUILDING

The site on which the Commonwealth Bank building stands today was purchased in 1939, although construction didn't commence until 1954 due to World War 2 and the post-war widening of Market Street. The eventual 12 storey design was therefore narrower than intended, resulting in three separate banking chambers occupying the lower ground, ground and first floors, all linked by escalators. This, along with the air-conditioning system (distributed to each level through perforated metal ceiling tiles), was an innovative feature for Sydney office buildings at the time.

The building is comprised of a two-storey podium, re-clad in polished granite in the 1990s, upon which sit ten floors of office space finished in the original sandstone. The Market Street elevation is dominated by an aluminium and glass curtain wall that projects from the facade within a sandstone frame. Each window is divided into unequal thirds with vertically ribbed spandrels adding to the textural nature of the surface.

The inclusion of public art was an important consideration from the beginning of the project and the three works originally displayed on the exterior survive intact. On the York Street elevation is a sandstone relief by sculptor Gerald Francis Lewers (1905-1962), whilst two works by Lyndon Dadswell (1908-1986) adorn the Market and George Street facades.

Not only was the Commonwealth Bank building the first major office tower to be constructed after World War 2, it is also the earliest remaining intact curtain wall structure in Sydney's CBD.

# TOWN HALL HOUSE

Since the 1880s the grand Town Hall building, sited on the corner of George and Druitt Streets, has been the seat of local government for the City of Sydney. By the 1970s, however, both the city and council had grown to such an extent that staff were scattered throughout the CBD. A new building was proposed to both centralise administration and improve the efficiency of the organisation.

Opened in 1977, Town Hall House is sited directly behind the Town Hall building on the corner of Druitt and Kent Streets. A stark contrast to its intricately decorated Victorian neighbour, the new building nonetheless reflected the architectural trends of its time with its complex stacked forms executed in the Brutalist manner.

Sitting on a multi-level podium the structure is essentially three main towers formed around a common service core. Rising to 25 floors, each tower structure is made up of two distinct blocks; a six storey 'base' on which sits a further block that extends up and projects out on blade-like columns. Blade forms feature throughout the structure, used as vertical sun-shading elements on the Kent Street elevation and throughout the podium structure. The windows are deeply recessed behind modular concave spandrel and frame elements.

Although unmistakably a product of 1970s Brutalism the architects were sensitive enough, given the spatial relationship to the older building, to give Town Hall House an acid-washed, buff-coloured aggregate finish that closely matches worn sandstone.

Be sure to check out
the impressive scale model
of the city on display in the
ground floor foyer of
Town Hall House.

### ✪ OF NOTE

#### 447 Kent Street / 1973

North of Town Hall House, down Kent Street, sits a 1970s office block not seemingly of its time. The tower rises above a double height entrance which is set back behind slim columns that continue in an expressed fashion up the entire height of the building. The curtain wall facade is composed of flush glazing and brown brick faced spandrels, a style and material choice that even by the mid-1960s was being largely superseded by heavier composite forms, receded windows and expressed sunshade elements. The result is a building that, compared to other structures of its era, has a quaint, old fashioned quality.

# ST ANDREWS HOUSE

Completed a year before Town Hall House, St Andrews House is another Brutalist product of the 1970s, although representing a more sober version of the style. Providing office space for a number of tenants, the building was primarily designed as the new home for St Andrews Cathedral School, a private Anglican co-educational institution that was established in 1885. The state's first high rise school, it occupies the ground, 5th, 6th, 7th and 8th floors and is attended by 1,100 students from kindergarten to Year 12.

The complex is made up of five staggered structures raised above a double height ground floor on columns. The columns form the sides of each facade, interlocking with the ends of the thick horizontal bands that form the spandrel elements on each level. Receded ribbon windows sit behind the spandrels, divided into 11 panels by brown mullions. The top levels display divided apertures matching the windows below and form a boundary for the school's rooftop play area, providing a safe, open space in a congested city location.

Finished in a rough aggregate, St Andrew's House is somewhat typical of the Brutalist style institutional architecture that could be found on campuses around Australia throughout the 1970s and 80s.

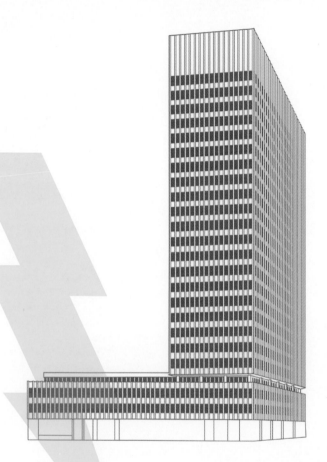

# SYDNEY ELECTRICITY BUILDING

The Sydney County Council building later renamed Sydney Electricity was opened in1968. It offered a sharp contrast in architectural style to its previous premises, the 1898 Queen Victoria Building. Sited on an elevated podium the 20 storey tower dramatically delineates the George and Bathurst Streets corner on which it is located.

Due to its black expressed mullion forms and dark grey cladding the building has often been referred to as a 'Miesien black box', alluding to the work of German/American architect Ludwig Mies van der Rohe. A pioneer of the corporate International Style, his skyscrapers (such as the Seagram Building, N.Y, 1958) often exhibited signature elements of dark glass and flat black painted structural expressions.

In 1961, shortly before construction was commenced on the new building, the City Council announced plans to demolish the Queen Victoria Building, a decision that faced surprisingly little opposition from the public. The council was unable, however, to legally evict the Sydney County Council at the time and, in the ensuing seven year delay, sentiments concerning built heritage dramatically changed, saving the QVB from the wrecking ball.

# SYDNEY MASONIC CENTRE

Freemasonry came to Australia shortly after the arrival of the First Fleet in 1788. Initially composed mainly of British soldiers, civilians soon swelled the membership ranks and the first official Grand Lodge was opened in Sydney in 1845.

Opening in 1974 as the new headquarters for the United Grand Lodge of NSW and the ACT, the Sydney Masonic Centre was as controversial to some as the secretive society it represented. Initially lacking the tower component (included in the original design but not added until 2004) the original squat, Brutalist structure was essentially a 30 metre high concrete podium encircled by a broad platform structure. This was supported both above and below by a series of triangular buttress forms.

Thirty years after completion the Grocon construction company, which now owned the airspace above the centre, went forward with a plan to build a tower atop the existing structure. Rejecting plans for a contemporary 'glass box', the company decided to use the original 35 floor Joseland Gilling design. Fully supported on the central lift core Civic Tower, with its upward tapering base, seems to balance precariously above the podium, giving it a sense of lightness belying its heavy concrete from.

## ✪ OF NOTE

### Roden Cutler House / 1975 / 24 Campbell Street

Walk south down Pitt Street for a block and turn right into Campbell Street and you will find a building named after decorated World War 2 veteran and long serving NSW Governor (1966-1981), Sir Roden Cutler. One for the die-hard Brutalist fans, the building is typical of the 1970s take on the style with a blank street frontage rising six floors above the entrance, abruptly transitioning to a heavily sun louvered tower.

Although critics remain steadfast in their attacks on 1970s era Brutalist architecture, fans of the style have praised the sympathetic stylistic unification of the Masonic Centre and, as Dr Harry Margalit, (architecture lecturer at the University of Sydney) has said, "Without doubt there will come a time when it is loved, and I think that time is not far away".

# ABOUT THE ARCHITECTS

If not for a request from his mother Harry Seidler may have continued to forge his career as an architect in the United States.

Born in Vienna to Jewish parents, 14 year old Seidler was sent to England soon after the Nazi occupation of Austria in 1938. In 1940 he was studying building and construction at Cambridgeshire Technical School when, because of his Austrian background, he was interned as an enemy alien on the Isle of Man. Shipped off to Quebec, Canada, his detention continued until October, 1941 when he was given probational release to study architecture at the University of Manitoba in Winnipeg. Graduating in 1944, Seidler was registered as an architect in 1945, becoming a Canadian citizen the following year.

He went on to study under Bauhaus founder Walter Gropius at the Harvard School of Design and subsequently worked for various architectural luminaries including Alvar Alto, Oscar Niemeyer and Marcel Breuer. An avid student of Modernist design principles from early on, the tuition and experience gained from these associations further cemented Seidler's convictions and ambitions concerning architecture and influenced many aspects of his own work. Breuer's 'bi-nuclear' house forms can be seen in Seidler's early timber domestic projects whilst sun shading elements and use of curved concrete forms, as utilised by Niemeyer, are evident in many of his later commercial towers.

Siedler's parents had migrated to Australia in 1946, settling in Sydney. In 1947 Rose Seidler contacted her son in New York with an interesting request: visit his parents and design a new home for them. The 'Rose Seidler House' as it has become known was completed in 1950 and, with its clearly Bauhaus-derived design philosophies expressed in bold cubic forms, sparked immediate interest amongst Sydneysiders. Awarded the Sulman Medal in 1951 (a prestigious New South Wales architectural prize) Seidler began receiving requests to design other peoples' homes and decided to stay in Australia indefinitely.

Focussing primarily on domestic architecture throughout the 1950s, the 1960s saw increasingly larger commissions starting with Blues Point Tower in 1961.

Founded in 1960 Harry Seidler and Associates went on to transform Sydney's CBD, constructing some of the city's most iconic buildings and re-shaping its urban spaces. Projects such as Australia Square (1967) and the MLC Centre (1975) altered the way people interacted with the city and, although designed around a thoroughly Modernist methodology, exhibited elements of sculptural sensitivity and regional practicality that were often hallmarks of Seidlers work.

Harry Seidler died in 2006 however his firm continues to make its mark on the built environment under the stewardship of his wife, Penelope.

When the NSW Government launched a design competition for a new opera house in 1955 it received 233 submissions from 32 countries. The eventual winner was a relatively obscure Danish architect whose work to date had consisted mainly of domestic projects around Scandinavia.

The son of a naval architect, Jorn Utzon was born in Copenhagen, where, in 1937, he attended the Royal Danish Academy of Fine Arts. After graduating in 1942 he moved to Stockholm, Sweden and worked with various Modernist architects including Arne Jacobsen and Poul Henningsen. Utzon travelled extensively following the end of the Second World War, beginning with Europe then onto Morocco, the United States and Mexico, before returning to Copenhagen in 1950 to start his own studio.

Completing a number of small projects throughout the 1950s, including his own home in Hellebaek (inspired by the work of Frank Lloyd Wright), Utzon set off again in 1957, visiting China, Japan and India before arriving in Australia to work on his most ambitious project yet.

From the beginning Utzon and his team were under enormous pressure from the state government to complete construction as early as possible. The state government feared that public opinion may baulk at the costs involved. This created less than ideal circumstances for such a grand project, especially one as complex and unique as the Opera House.

In 1965 a new state government was voted in, one that was less than enthusiastic about the project.

The incoming Minister for Public Works, David Hughes, clashed with Utzon over administrative, design and cost issues, which eventually resulted in the architect's resignation and departure in February, 1966. The role was taken over by Government Architect Peter Hall who oversaw the completion of the structure including the interiors, although these were not done to Utzon's original designs.

Jorn Utzon never returned to Australia. He spent the following decades working primarily in Denmark, producing a variety of domestic and commercial buildings, all of which reflect the well-travelled architect's eclectic Modernist influences and cultural experiences.

During the 1990's, in an effort at reconciliation with Utzon, he was approached by the Sydney Opera House Trust with a request for his involvement in any future alterations to the building. In 2004 a room was rebuilt to an original design by the architect and named in his honour. The Utzon Room features natural timber and bare concrete finishes and is decorated with a colourful 14 metre tapestry of the architect's own design.

When Utzon was awarded architecture's highest honour, the Pritzker Architecture Prize, in 2003, the citation read: 'There is no doubt that the Sydney Opera House is his masterpiece. It is one of the great iconic buildings of the 20th century, an image of great beauty that has become known throughout the world – a symbol for not only a city, but a whole country and continent.'

# GLOSSARY

Bays: The spaces between posts, columns, or buttresses in the length of a building

Brutalism: An architectural style that emerged in the 1950s utilising raw concrete ('beton brut' in French) as the building material of choice.

Colonnade: A repeating series of columns supporting an upper structure

Curtain wall: The outer covering, or facade, of a building that is non-structural. New advances in aluminium and glass technology during the 1950s enabled the lightweight glass curtain walls that are ubiquitous on commercial buildings of this era

Elliptical: Oval in shape

Facade: An exterior side of a building, usually, but not always, the front

Floorplate: A concrete slab that forms an individual floor of a skyscraper

Hi-Tech: Also known as Structural Expressionism, a late Modern architectural style that incorporates cutting edge construction technologies and materials. Such buildings often reveal internal structures and forms externally.

Mullion: The vertical structural element forming a division between units of windows.

Plaza: An open urban public space

Podium: A platform used to raise a structure

Ribbon Windows: A series of windows set side by side to form a continuous band horizontally across a facade

Setback: The distance that a building's frontage is located from the street line

Spandrel: In reference to modern, multi-storeyed buildings, an infill panel between the top of one window and the sill or base of the one above. On 1950s curtain wall designs the spandrel was often a pane of opaque coloured glass.

Terrazzo: A composite material used extensively during the 1950s and 60s in both domestic and commercial architecture as floor and wall surfacing. Originally invented by Venetian construction workers, terrazzo consists of marble, quartz, granite or glass chips combined with a binding agent. The mixture is either poured on site, then ground and polished or pre-fabricated as tiles which can be laid in the traditional manner.

Truss: A series of straight members joined together in triangular forms to provide structural support

# SYDNEY TIMELINE
## 1945-1990

**1945** The Sydney-Hobart yacht race is held for the first time. The winner is 'Rani'.

**1947** Population of greater Sydney reaches 1,484,434.

**1951** Waverley Council bans the bikini swimsuit on its beaches.

**1954** A Telex (teleprinter exchange) service is introduced to the city.

**1955** Six o'clock closing of hotels in NSW ends. Bars are allowed to open till 10pm.

**1956** Channel TCN-9 Sydney launches Australia's first regular television service.

**1958** Cahill Expressway is opened.

**1961** Trams in Sydney stop running.

**1964** Bernard 'Midget' Farrelly wins the World Surfing Championship at Manly beach.

**1966** Jorn Utzon resigns as designer of the Sydney Opera House.

**1971** Green Bans are first imposed on building development in Sydney to protect heritage buildings.

**1973** Sydney Opera House opens.

**1976** Nude bathing is allowed on two Sydney beaches.

**1977** Australia's worst railway disaster occurs when a commuter train from the Blue Mountains crashes into a concrete bridge at Granville, Sydney; 83 people are killed and many injured by the falling bridge.

**1984** Hyde Park Barracks are restored and converted to a museum of social history.

**1988** The First Fleet re-enactment vessels arrive at Botany Bay as part of Australia's bicentennial celebrations.

**1990** Opera singer Joan Sutherland gives the final performance of her career at the Sydney Opera House.

# THE WALK

The Footpath Guide to
Sydney Modern architecture
takes approximately
two hours to complete.